The Murder of Mingo Jack

THE MURDER OF
MINGO JACK

NEW JERSEY'S ONLY NINETEENTH CENTURY LYNCHING

✣ *James M. Stone* ✣

iUniverse, Inc.
New York   Bloomington

The Murder of Mingo Jack
New Jersey's only nineteenth century lynching

iUniverse books may be ordered through booksellers or by contacting:

iUniverse
1663 Liberty Drive
Bloomington, IN 47403
www.iuniverse.com
1-800-Authors (1-800-288-4677)

Because of the dynamic nature of the Internet, any Web addresses or
links contained in this book may have changed since publication and
may no longer be valid. The views expressed in this work are solely those
of the author and do not necessarily reflect the views of the publisher, and
the publisher hereby disclaims any responsibility for them.

ISBN: 978-1-4502-1320-2 (sc)
ISBN: 978-1-4502-1321-9 (ebk)

Printed in the United States of America

iUniverse rev. date: 02/23/2010

To my third Great Grandfather, Freeman Stone, who in 1882 came from England to America to start a new life.

Table of Contents

Acknowledgments ix

Introduction xi

Chapter 1   Two Families in Eatontown 1

Chapter 2   Two Awful Crimes 7

Chapter 3   Summarily Condemned 17

Chapter 4   Tell All That Happened 25

Chapter 5   A Friendly Enemy 41

Chapter 6   They All Took Their Oaths 59

Chapter 7   Voluntary Confession. 67

Chapter 8   Revenge 73

Chapter 9   Out Of Sight, Out Of Mind. 81

Bibliography 85

Acknowledgments

First and foremost I would like to thank Helen Pike and Glenn Vogel for their book "*Images of American; Eatontown and Fort Monmouth*". In the spring of 2008 I was reading through the book when I first came across the story of Mingo Jack. I spoke with both Ms. Pike and Mr. Vogel and they were able to get me started with where to look for information on this topic. I would like to thank my mother, June Stone, for being the first to read and critique my book, my aunt, Emily Humphries, for assisting with some editing, and my cousin, Charlie Thomason, for illustrating the cover.

Both the Monmouth County Archives and the Monmouth County Historical Association provided me with a wealth of information to help write this book. Specifically I would like to thank Gary Saretzky and Mary Ann Kiernan for their help. It was Mr. Saretzky's work on this story where I got a lot of my information from. Special thanks goes to Dr. Richard Fernicola, for his tireless research on the 1916 Shark Attacks and subsequent book on the subject that first gave me an appreciation for local history. I would like to thank George Joynson for his book *Murders in Monmouth* and the belief that I would one day turn my research into a book. I would also like to thank the Eatontown Historical Society for their help as well as the Middletown Public Library for putting *The Red Bank Registry* newspaper online. Finally, I would like to thank the New Jersey Hall of Records, the Monmouth County Library, the Asbury Park Public Library, Shrewsbury Historical Society, and the Monmouth University Library for their help.

Introduction

Monmouth County's first English resident was a woman by the name of Penelope Pristin. She was traveling by boat from England on her way to New Amsterdam (New York City) with her husband. They got caught in a bad storm and the boat ran aground about twenty miles south of the city, near present day Sandy Hook. They were soon attacked by Lenapi Indians who killed Penelope's husband and left her severely injured. Penelope ran to an area of woods and hid from the Indians for days. The Indians later found her, but instead of killing Penelope, they decided to spare her life and sell her to the English. She settled in upper Monmouth County and later married Richard Stout. They resided in the newly formed village of Middletown. Legend has it that she had ten children and lived to be one hundred and ten years old. She had over one hundred descendants who later settled in the area and would become the area's first English residents. More people soon settled in Middletown and in 1675 Monmouth County was given its name by Col. Lewis Morris of Tinton Falls.

By the late nineteenth century Monmouth County, New Jersey was a place that was well-known around the country. Situated in the central part of the state it was located near the major cities of New York, Philadelphia, and Atlantic City. The bordering New Jersey shore attracted people from all over the northeast including many celebrities and politicians. Seven different presidents vacationed or resided in the Monmouth County area during the late nineteenth and early twentieth century. In the 1870's President Grant had a vacation home in the town of Long Branch.

In 1881, then thirtieth President of the United States, James Garfield spent his last days at Franklyn Cottage in Elberon after he was struck by an assassin's bullet. His staff had hoped that the sea air would help him recover from his wounds. Unfortunately President Garfield passed away on September 15, 1881 in Elberon. The Governor of New Jersey, Woodrow Wilson also had his home in Long Branch New Jersey. When he became president he still vacationed at the New Jersey shore quite often with his family. During a bizarre series of shark attacks that occurred along the Jersey shore in 1916, President Wilson turned the Trust building located in Asbury Park into his summer Whitehouse. During that same time his cabinet also had meetings in nearby convention hall in order to determine what to do about the "shark problem".

It was also during this time that Edward Hazard had his Ketchup factory in the historic town of Shrewsbury.

Once a thriving business; Hazard was in competition with Heinz ketchup and is credited with helping get Tabasco sauce well known. Located just below Shrewsbury and about five miles from Long Branch was another Monmouth County village known as Eatontown.

In 1670 Thomas Eaton came from Rhode Island and settled in the area which would later be known as Eatontown. He was the first permanent European resident. He built a successful grist mill along Parkers's Creek and the area around it began to prosper. Mr. Eaton ran the mill until he passed away in 1688 when his wife took over operations. The mill would change hands over half a dozen times and not be torn down until 1927, all the while bringing commerce into the area.

More people began to settle in the area because of the proximity to the nearby Jersey shore. The center of town was just south of the Parker's Creek (then known as Mill Pond) and contained many retail establishments. In 1870 Monmouth Racetrack was built just a half mile from the town and the summer tourism began to explode. People from all over would travel by train to watch the horses' race. Some famous people also made Monmouth Racetrack a summer destination; these included "Diamond Jim" Brady, Presidents Grover Cleveland and Ulysses S. Grant, John Pierpoint Morgan, Lillian Russel, Alfred Lord Tennyson, Bret Harte, and many others. In 1873 Eatontown was officially declared a township, named for its founder Mr. Eaton. The main road which traveled through the town was known as Poplar Road. The road extended north to Red Bank and went as far south as the village of Poplar which was located in the township of Ocean. The road itself had a lot of history associated with it because it was once part of the Burlington trail that was used by the Lenapi Indians. By the 1880's Eatontown had become a well established area with a population of close to 3,000 people. But with the exception of the summer tourism from Monmouth Park, Eatontown would remain relatively quiet in the winter. However in March of 1886 that peacefulness would be suddenly interrupted by a crime that would gain the attention of the entire state and bring out the worst in some of the residents in Monmouth County.

Chapter 1

Two Families in Eatontown

Mr. Thomas Stewart Herbert was a working class man who was very protective over his family. Born in 1833 in Ocean County New Jersey, Mr. Herbert was raised by his parents, Henry and Mary Herbert in the town of Brick; just five miles from the Jersey shore. Mr. Herbert was descended from the large Herbert family of Ocean County which came to the region in the 1700's. The town of Herbertsville which is located just off the present day Garden State Parkway near mile marker 91 is now named for the family. Around 1855 Thomas met and married Sarah Herbert in Bricktown. Over the next ten years the couple had seven Children; John, Martha, Juliette, Angelina, Joseph, George and Thomas.

In 1881 Mr. Herbert and his family moved from the Bricktown area and settled in Monmouth County, New Jersey. They bought a house two and a half miles south of Eatontown on Poplar Road. The two story house was somewhat rundown and located just fifty yards from

Maps Saw Mill. Across the street from their house was a large pond which was part of Whalepond Brook. It powered the mill that the Maps owned and later became known as Mapes Pond. Bordering the pond were also two ice houses which were used by both the Maps and the Herberts. Mr. Herbert worked as a carpenter in the area and did odd jobs around the county to earn any extra money he could to help support his family.

By 1886 three of the Herbert's older children had been married and left home, however one of Mr. Herbert's daughters, twenty four year old Angelina, was still at home, sick, and unable to live a normal life. In the early 1880's she had contracted tuberculosis and had mostly been an invalid since then. Sometimes she felt well enough to wander outside and occasionally was able to join the family at the Branchburg Methodist Church where they worshipped every Sunday. Angelina was cared for by her parents and younger brothers who were still living at home. They were obviously very protective over her and her condition and affectionately referred to her as "Anna". *The Red Bank Registry* describe her physical appearance the following way, "Miss Herbert is tall, slender, fair complexioned, with a hectic flush and an oval face. She has rather prominent cheek bones, a small mouth, round chin, straight nose, hazel eyes, and a low straight forehead above which clusters a wealth of chestnut hair". Angelina was a smart woman and was well spoken. She had very simple tastes and loved her family very much.

Just a half mile north of the Herbert house lived the Johnson family. The head of the family was Samuel Johnson; more well-known as Mingo Jack. He was born sometime around 1820 in Colts Neck, New Jersey. His parents, Thomas and Elizabeth Johnson, abandoned him at an early age and he was raised by the family of Samuel Laird. The Laird family has a rich history in Monmouth County. They created Laird's Applejack Whiskey and gave George Washington the recipe in the 1700's. The whiskey soon became very popular around the country. The Lairds owned a large amount of farmland, some of which is still located today on Highway 537 in Colts Neck as well as their brewery which is one of the oldest in the country. Since Samuel was an African American man in a time when slavery was still legal in New Jersey, he was used as a servant by the Laird family. They owned a lot of race horses and seeing that Samuel was quite short and stocky they chose him to be a jockey. He would race the families' horses at Monmouth Racetrack. Samuel won a big race with a Philadelphia horse that just happened to be named "Chief Mingo". For the rest of his life Samuel Johnson would be referred to by the name of the horse which he had won the race with. Mingo Jack continued to work for the Lairds well into his twenties as a slave. In the 1840's Mingo was officially emancipated and no longer had to serve the family. By some accounts the Laird family was glad to see him go because he had become quite uncontrollable and unruly.

Newspaper article from 1838 advertising the race horse "Mingo". It is believed this is where Mingo Jack got his name. (Courtesy Monmouth Democrat)

Mingo Jack moved to Middletown where he began to work for Thomas Field for a number of years. It was during this time when he met and married his wife Lucy. They soon had a son named George and a daughter named Henrietta. Apparently the couple had a number of other children as well; however there is no record of them aside from casual mentions in various newspapers. Mingo also worked for another family in Middletown as a farmer. It was here where he began to establish an unfavorable reputation. Mingo was accused of sexually assaulting the families' two young daughters while outside farming. He was beaten by the daughters' father and fired from his job in Middletown. Whether he was ever arrested for this crime is unknown, however a few years later Mingo was back at Monmouth Racetrack working as a rudder and working part time in a butcher shop in Eatontown. Mingo Jack soon settled in a two story house that was situated about two miles south of Eatontown, on Poplar Road. Each floor was said to have only been thirteen square feet. It was so small that it could barely hold his entire family inside and was more of a cabin then an actual house. The family leased the home from William Conover, who lived in Red Bank.

On October fifteenth 1865 Mingo Jack was arrested for an assault against Andrew Emmons. Mingo Jack spent nearly six months in jail for the assault. However it appears as though Mingo was simply trying to defend his wife Lucy. Mr. Emmons was charged with assault against Lucy Johnson however he was eventually acquitted by a grand jury in December of 1865. It is strange that Mingo Jack would be sent to jail for defending his wife and the attacker would be acquitted for the attack.

In the early 1880's things began to get worse for Mingo and his family. His wife Lucy, well into her sixties, had become ill and bedridden. His daughter, now forty years old, had three children of her own which were born out of wedlock. The family was extremely poor and the town had to help them out by giving them financial assistance from their "poor fund". Despite Mingo's work at the Monmouth Park Racetrack and as a butcher in Eatontown, he was still in desperate need for money. In the fall of 1884 Mingo Jack decided to hold up a carriage on a dirt road near his house. Mingo demanded from the man driving the carriage all the money that he had. The man pretended to comply with Mingo's request but instead pulled out a gun and shot Mingo in the leg. The police in Eatontown never got involved in the matter because they believed that Mingo had gotten what he deserved, however this incident left Mingo unable to work for nearly three months and continued to tarnish his reputation in Eatontown. In 1885 Mingo Jack claimed the he was assaulted by twenty five year old Eatontown resident Joseph Anderson, however it appears that no charges were ever filed. Mr. Anderson would eventually have to deal with more charges concerning Mingo Jack.

Although he was sixty six years old by 1886, Mingo was still in great health. It was said that he could outrun men twenty years younger than him. He was short and perhaps only weighed one hundred and twenty pounds. However he had a massive amount of upper body strength and didn't have a grey hair on his head. In early March of 1886 Mingo had gotten a job near Maps' Pond chopping wood at James Crummel's house. To get there Mingo would have to walk over Maps pond bridge and directly in front of the Herbert's house. It was here where Angelina Herbert would occasionally see Mingo Jack from out of the front window of her house. No one knew it at the time but these circumstances would later prove to be disastrous.

Chapter 2

Two Awful Crimes

On Friday March 5, 1886 Angelina Herbert was feeling better than usual and had received permission from her parents to visit Jackson Brown and his family to return a tin baking dish that had been borrowed. The families had been friends for years and both Thomas and Sarah Herbert figured that the time out of the house would be good for Angelina. This was a decision they would later regret. Jackson Brown's house was nearly a mile away and you had to travel down a desolate path and through a wooded area in order to get to the Brown's house.

Angelina left her house at about four twenty in the evening and started her journey. She headed north on Poplar Road crossed over the bridge near Maps's Pond, and turned right on a desolate stagecoach road that lead to the Brown's house. When she was about halfway there she was suddenly hit twice with a red oak stick; once in the shoulder and once on the head. The force of the blows threw Angelina to the ground and she was nearly knocked unconscious. In a daze she had the strength to turn around just as she was seized by the neck and began to be choked. He attacker then picked her up and dragged her off the road into the woods.

In an interview conducted by a local newspaper called *The Red Bank Registry* later the next day, Angelina described what happened next; "He asked me if I knew Mingo Jack and told me that he lived in Eatontown. I knew him the moment I put my eyes upon him, but I was afraid that if I told him so that he would murder me, so I shook my head no. I attempted to scream, and he said that if I made a noise he would kill me. He choked me so hard that I could not make an audible sound and I soon became unconscious. He then accomplished his purpose and left me on the ground".

Angelina had been brutally beaten and raped and the attacker had fled. When she regained consciousness she somehow managed to gather enough strength to crawl the rest of the way to the Brown's house. Once there she told Mrs. Brown what had happened to her. A young man by the name of Al Lefferson who was at the Brown house when Angelina arrived, heard the story and took off on his horse towards the Herbert house to notify them of the attack.

Upon hearing the story of the attack, Mrs. Herbert became hysterical. She knew that Angelina was suffering quite a bit already from tuberculosis and was very upset that yet another tragedy had befallen her daughter. Mr. Herbert heard the story and immediately rode over to Jackson Brown's house in order to bring Angelina home. He had taken his son, Joseph, with him to the Jackson's house.

The other two brothers, twenty year old Thomas and eighteen year old George, got their guns out and set off in the woods to look for Mingo. They were persuaded by Mrs. Herbert not to kill Mingo if they happened to come across him. She was also smart enough to hide her husband's rifle, because from the anger in his eyes she knew he was capable of killing Mingo Jack. Mr. Herbert soon returned home with Angelina and then immediately set out on his horse up Poplar Drive in order to bring the stricken girl help. In the center of Eatontown Mr. Herbert managed to locate Dr. William Beach and Justice of the Peace John H. Edwards. Dr. Beach went to the Herbert home while Justice Edwards summoned Constable Hermann Liebenthall to go and arrest Mingo Jack without a warrant. It was also reported that Justice Edwards had to disarm Mr. Herbert of the pistol he was carrying because Herbert had threatened to take Mingo Jack's life if he saw him.

Around six o'clock in the evening, Constable Liebenthall and Mr. Herbert were making their way down Poplar Drive to arrest Mingo Jack. When they went into Mingo Jack's house they found him sitting at the table eating dinner with his family. By some accounts he was simply sitting by the fire with his coat off. In either case the Constable informed him that he was under arrest and Mingo replied, "What for?" In a rage Mr. Herbert shouted back at him, "You know what for!" and proceeded to curse at him.

Just as a fight between the two was about to take place, Constable Liebenthall stepped in between the men and ordered Mr. Herbert to wait outside. It is unclear why the Constable would have allowed Mr. Herbert to actually enter the house to begin with. Mingo Jack quickly submitted to arrest but denied having anything to do with the rape and beating of Angelina Herbert.

Mingo's daughter, Henrietta Johnson, followed her father outside and watched Mingo placed into the wagon. There she ran into Mr. Herbert who was still very angry and according to her said "Don't worry he'll never trouble you again".

Meanwhile Mr. Herbert's sons; having not had any success finding Mingo, had waited in the bushes outside his house with shotguns ready to shoot him incase he tried to make an escape. However as soon as they saw that he was under arrest they decided it was best to go home.

At the same time Dr. Beach had arrived at the Herbert house and found Angelina to be in a great amount of pain and saw that she was suffering. He gave her a large injection of morphine to calm her down. He was able to confirm that she had been raped and beaten. In his report he noted that she had swelling on her head from where she had been hit from the club.

Justice Edwards soon arrived at the house and wrote down Angelina's account of what had happened. She confirmed to him that it was indeed Mingo Jack who had attacked her. Dr. Beach cared for Angelina as best as he could, and as soon as he finished his report and Mr. Herbert returned home, Dr Beach left the family for the night. Justice Edwards also arrived at the house to take a statement from Angelina as to what had happened for his own report.

After a brief stop at his Constable Liebenthall's house, Mingo Jack was taken to the Eatontown lockup and placed inside. The Eatontown lockup was located on Mill Pond in the center of town, about five hundred feet to the south of where Thomas Eaton's mill was located. The Eatontown Lockup was generally used as a temporary facility for drunk and disorderly persons and not for someone who was being accused of a serious crime. It was a small building only twelve feet wide and nine feet high. Inside the building were two cells, each one surrounded by bars. Each cell had a small bed and with just enough room between the bed and the bars to stand. There was a glass window on the lockup that was also covered with bars. The door was made of heavy oak with a padlock on it to keep the prisoners from escaping, or perhaps to keep the people from the outside from coming in. On the way to the lockup Mingo saw Thomas Wheeler. The men exchanged words and Mingo asked Wheeler if he could vouch for his whereabouts earlier in the day. Mr.

Wheeler said he could but added that Mingo was lucky he had been caught otherwise he might already be dead. By some accounts Mingo Jack once again denied having anything to do with the beating and rape of Angelina Herbert saying he had no idea what was going on.

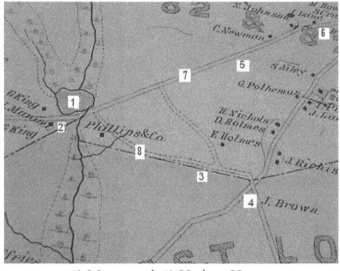

1) Maps pond. 2) Herbert House.
3) Approximate Spot where Angelina was attacked.
4) Jackson Brown's house. 5) Mingo Jack's house.
6) Dr Beach's house. 7) Poplar Road (today Hwy 35)
8) Stage coach road used by Angelina.
(Photo courtesy of Wolverton Atlas)

News soon spread around town of the attack on Angelina Herbert. There was outrage and a number of people gathered around the lockup to yell insults at Mingo Jack and threaten to hang him. However Mingo didn't reply to the threats and didn't seem to take them all that seriously.

There was discussion about Mingo Jack's past crimes, such as the abuse of the farmer's two daughters in Middletown and the time he had tried to hold up the man near Eatontown. Another story was told of how Mingo had been standing in the woods near a man's house for "no good reason". The man sent his wife out to investigate the matter and Mingo grabbed her by the arm. The farmer saw this and ran out of house and began punching and kicking Mingo who then promised to "mend his ways". Most people thought he was a bad man and believed that he should be hung.

The crowd eventually got tired of standing around the lockup though and went back home. Around nine o'clock a friend of Mingo Jack's named Jeremiah Thompson went to the lockup and spoke with Mingo. Thompson reiterated that many people in the town wanted to see Mingo dead and that they were threatening to hang him. Showing no fear, Mingo said to his friend, "Let them kill me and be damned". At around 10pm Constable Liebenthall returned to the lockup to check on Mingo Jack. The Constable had been at a democratic primary in Oceanport and came back to make sure Mingo was safe. They had a brief conversation and Mingo mentioned the threats against his life but didn't seem to be too overly concerned about it. The Constable assured Mingo that there would be no attack against him. The Constable then built a fire in the lockup in order to keep Mingo warm for the night and left. This is the last time anyone would admit to having seen Mingo Jack alive.

A little before midnight a crowd estimated between twenty and forty people arrived at the Eatontown lockup with one mission: to kill Mingo Jack. Much of what happened there is based on speculation, physical evidence, and witness testimony that would later be taken. However, what is certain is that it was a horrific crime.

One man was hoisted up on another's shoulders and attempted to shoot through the glass window at Mingo. At least three shots were fired into the lockup however they all missed Mingo and lodged into the wood inside the lockup. The mob then decided that the only way they would be able to get to Mingo was to break down the door. A crowbar was obtained by breaking into a nearby shed owned by Samuel Billings and the crowd smashed open the door of the lockup. They entered Mingo Jack's cell and began to beat him with various objects they had obtained. Mingo fought like a madman for his life, shouting "Murder!" "Murder!" in hopes that someone might come to his rescue. Mingo pushed hard to get to the lockup door and pass the crowd; throwing blows at various people in hopes he could stun enough of them to make an exit. Each time the crowd pushed him back and continued the beating. Mingo was able to escape the cell he was in and run to the cell on the opposite side of the room in a vain attempt to flee the attackers. Pools of blood began to collect on the floor, some of it was Mingo's and some of it was his attackers. Mingo's eyes were gouged out at a certain point. The attackers delivered two heavy blows to his head and Mingo fell to the ground either unconscious or dead. A rope was obtained and the crowd tied his hands behind his back. They then strung a rope around his neck and hung him from the lockup door. After the lynching was complete, some people in the crowd took the instruments that were used to beat Mingo and broke the ice that was on mill pond. They needed water in order to clean Mingo's blood off themselves or perhaps clean off some of their own blood.

Wolverton Atlas from 1889 showing the spot where Mingo Jack was lynched (photo courtesy of author).

Chapter 3

Summarily Condemned

S aturday Morning March 6, 1886 at six o'clock in the morning, two African American boys were walking along Mill Pond. They had setup muskrat traps along the creek banks and were checking to see if they had caught any game. The boys turned down West Street near the railroad tracks when suddenly they caught sight of the disfigured body of Mingo Jack hanging in the doorway of the lockup. Frightened by what they saw, they ran into town to notify a man by the name of Dick Stevens who contacted Justice Edwards and Constable Liebenthal.

These men went to the lockup and once they had seen what was done, contacted Coroner R.T Smith of Red Bank and Coroner W.M T VanWoert of Long Branch. Coroner Smith soon arrived and cut down the lifeless body of Mingo Jack and carried him inside the lockup so that a crowd of people wouldn't gather and see the body. Coroner Smith sent for Dr. Beach who had just examined Angelina Herbert the day before. Dr. Beach examined the body of Mingo Jack and determined that his skull and been broken in three different places and it was likely that he had been killed from the blows and not as a result of the strangulation from the lynching. Inside the lockup they found three wooden clubs that were covered in blood and a felt hat that had been torn to pieces.

Constable Liebenthal had noticed that when he locked up Mingo Jack the night before that he was not wearing at hat, so it was believed that the hat came from one of the attackers and was gathered as evidence. On Mingo's body they found a logbook with records of his day's work, an empty pocketbook, and a red handkerchief. All these items were covered in a massive amount of blood, as was the entire floor of the lockup.

Spot where Mingo Jack was lynched.
The lockup is to the left of the photo.
(Photo courtesy of the Eatontown Historical Society)

Meanwhile news was spreading throughout the town that Mingo Jack had been hung. The people of Eatontown generally believed that Mingo had gotten what he deserved. Many reflected on the assault of Angelina and came to the conclusion that Mingo Jack was a better citizen dead then he was alive. However there was also quite a bit of speculation amongst the townspeople as to who could have done such a thing. There was so much anger over Angelina's assault that almost anyone could have been considered a suspect.

The primary suspects were, of course, Mr. Herbert and his sons. Out of everyone, they had the biggest motive to commit such a crime. Early that morning Mr. Herbert was near his house getting ice when a young boy named Hayes notified him of the lynching. Mr. Herbert was no doubt glad that Mingo Jack was no longer a threat, however he wanted to make clear that his whole family had been at home the entire night before.

Back at the lockup, evidence was being still being collected. Coroner Smith instructed Constable Liebenthal to go into town and find twelve jurors to preside over the upcoming coroner's inquest. As instructed, the Constable found twelve jurors, mostly middle aged and elderly men. Their names were Lyttleton White, Thomas White, Joseph Herbert (no relation to the Herbert family), Robertson Smith, Chas Farrington, Henry Corlies, Joseph Johnston, William Brown, John Hulick, John Sickles, Felix McCarthy, and Walter Reynolds. The jurors met at the town's large hotel located at the corner of Main Street and Poplar Road at ten o'clock. There they were swore in and led to the lockup to view the body of Mingo Jack. Once the body had been viewed it was taken by Mingo Jack's daughter and brought to his home.

The story quickly hit the local papers. It was front page news on *The Red Bank Registry*, *Monmouth Democrat*, and *Eatontown Advisor*. *The Asbury Park Press*, only a few years old at the time, ran a headline entitled "Two Awful Crimes". Even papers from New York City and Philadelphia were running stories on the lynching. *The New York Times* and *New York Sun* both ran front page stories as well. Editor of *The Eatontown Advisor*, Jacob B. Coffin, wrote an editorial that said the entire town approved of the lynching. The editorial read in part, "The people of Eatontown sanction the removal of Samuel Johnson (Mingo Jack). They are satisfied that he deserved his fate. They are glad that men of nerve were found to represent them, and they do not want them convicted of and punished for a crime which, in light of the circumstances which led to it, is not a crime but just retribution". *The Red Bank Registry* seemed to somewhat approve of this position by calling Mr. Coffin's editorial "clever and concise". However *The Monmouth Democrat* took the opposite position on the matter. The paper condemned Mr. Coffin's position and said the people of Eatontown should be ashamed of themselves. In a long editorial that appeared in *The Monmouth Democrat*, they wrote "If the miserable Negro is summarily condemned because he did not restrain his unlawful and criminal propensities, what judgment shall we render against these intelligent men who laid unlawful hands on him?". There was also a statement made that Constable Liebenthal violated the law by placing Mingo Jack in a temporary lockup instead of bringing him to the more secure jail in Freehold. The battle lines were drawn between *The Red Bank Registry* and *The Monmouth Democrat*. The feud between the two papers would continue through the trial and for years to come.

On Sunday March 7, 1886 a vigil was held at Mingo Jack's cabin. His body was laid out and people came to pay their respects to him. A reporter from *The New York Times* described the body as being in relatively good condition for the crime committed. However they said pieces of cotton were in place where Mingo's eyes had been. You could also clearly see where the rope had been placed around his neck.

One of the mourners heading to the cabin was traveling along Poplar Road when they stopped and asked Charles Boyce for directions. Mr. Boyce said to them, "We have sent Mingo Jack as far to hell as we can get him on earth." This statement can give you an idea of what the opinion of the situation was like around town. Originally Mingo was going to be buried on Sunday; however Dr. Beach wanted to perform another autopsy on him in order to better determine the cause of death so the burial was delayed for another day.

Mingo Jack death certificate. Cause of death
is listed as "compound fracture caused by
person or persons unknown to Coroner"
(Courtesy of the Trenton State Archives)

As scheduled, the funeral for Mingo Jack was
held the following day at ten in the morning. A
crowd gathered at his cabin on Poplar Road to pay
their respects. The house was so small that only

about fifteen people could fit inside. Mingo's widow, Lucy Johnson lay in a cot that was in a loft of the cabin. She was guarded by her son, George, because she was apparently delirious and unaware of what was happening. Coroner's Smith's brother was the officiating undertaker and the only white man in the crowd. Mingo's body was placed in a cheap pine box in preparation for burial. However, Mingo Jack's stepson, William Hendrickson objected to this and said "old Mingo should be sent into the next world in a decent coffin at least." Mr. Hendrickson shouted and kicked the pine box and was finally able to get Mingo placed into a coffin made of white wood stained to look like black walnut. Mr. Hendrickson figured that since the county was paying for the funeral, he might as well try and get a more expensive coffin. The body was loaded onto a wagon, which had been provided by George Hance of Shrewsbury, and brought to the Macedonia colored church where services took place. The pastor, Reverend John Hammet, spoke of Mingo Jack's life but did not mention the crime that had happened. Two hymns were sung; "Watts Hymn" and "The Final Account". After the sermon was over it was reported that Mingo Jack's daughter, Henrietta Johnson, fainted. Nearly seventy-five people followed on foot from the church to the cemetery. Mingo was brought to the pauper's burial ground just south of Eatontown, called Locust Grove Cemetery. He was buried in an unmarked grave in the southeast corner of the cemetery. Most people did not stay long at the burial because they wanted to get a seat at Hall's Hotel, where the coroner's inquest into his murder was about to begin.

Chapter 4

Tell All That Happened

Hall's Hotel, formerly known as the Wheeler Hotel was located in the center of Eatontown at the corner of Main and Broad Street. The hotel, owned by Peter Hall would take center stage as the inquest into the death of Mingo Jack began. In the center of the small room stood two tables pushed together. Sitting at these tables were Coroner William Van Woert and Coroner Robert Smith. Sitting next to them was Assistant District Attorney John W. Swartz and lawyer James Steen.

Mr. Steen was well known in Eatontown and owned a number of buildings including one near the lockup. These men were all part of the prosecution during the inquest. On the opposite end of the room sat the jury. A piano stool was use as the bench witnesses would sit on as they testified. The inquest would be nothing short of a farce. Most people did not believe that the matter should even be looked into and saw the entire inquest as a joke. Over ninety witnesses would be called in during the course of the six day inquest. Many of them would be drunk on the stand and blatantly lie about what had occurred the night of Mingo Jack's lynching. In fact, the alcohol consumption got so bad that when Peter Hall submitted his bill for the use of the hotel, it was decreased with the excuse that he had made so much money off the sale of alcohol. Other incapable or incompetent witnesses would take the stand and offer little of any value to the case. *The New York Times* characterized one witness after he left the stand as being "so deaf he could barely hear a question, and so dumb he couldn't answer one." Each witness was paid fifty cents for their testimony, so many simply wanted to testify in order to receive the money.

I will spare the reader from having to read about testimony from witnesses that had no bearing on the case. However, there were competent witnesses and from the chaos emerged some important clues and theories as to what could have really taken place on the night of March fifth. Ultimately, it would be questionable as to whether or not Mingo Jack was even guilty of the assault on Angelina Herbert.

At ten in the morning on Monday, March eight, 1886 the inquest began. The first witness that was called was Justice John Edwards. He retold the story of how he had been contacted by Mr. Herbert about the assault on Angelina. Edwards said that Mr. Herbert gave him the impression that he would have shot Mingo Jack on sight, so Justice Edwards took Herbert's gun from him before Edwards allowed Herbert to leave with Constable Liebenthal. Edwards also stated how he went to the Herbert home to take the complaint of Angelina. He admitted that Mingo Jack was arrested without a warrant, but that the warrant was later obtained the following day.

Edwards described the scene at the lockup on Saturday and testified that a man by the name of William Kelly had asked to see the rope that was used to hang Mingo Jack. According to the Justice, Mr. Kelly then admitted to him that it was the same rope he had tied a hangmen's knot in at Allen's Saloon on the previous night. With this small piece of testimony a story began to take shape. Allen's saloon was located just across the street from the lockup at the corner of Broad Street and Railroad Avenue. Owned by James Allen, the saloon was a local hangout for many of the towns people. Apparently a number of men had been drinking there the previous night just before the lynching took place. This saloon and the events that transpired in the saloon that night would later become the focal point of the entire trial.

The most obvious person to call to the stand next was William Kelly himself. He was a middle aged man with red hair and a long red beard who frequented the local Eatontown taverns and was known by many as a drunk. He had a wealthy wife who supported him and his drinking habit so there was no need for him to have a job. As Kelly sat on the witness stand the coroners asked Justice Edwards if this was the same William Kelly who had made the confession about the rope and Edwards replied that it was. Mr. Kelly suddenly jumped from the stool and said, "If it's about the rope that went out of Allen's you want me here for, there was no knot in that rope!" Mr. Kelly was then excused from the witness stand and denied the fifty cent payment because he was not sworn in. It is unclear why the prosecution would not let him to continue to testify under oath. Perhaps they believed he was too drunk or otherwise incapable of testifying.

As the day continued there were more witnesses called to the stand. Constable Liebenthal talked about the arrest of Mingo. He said he did not handcuff Mingo or any prisoners for that matter because Liebenthal had a chest that measured fifty three inches around. Liebenthal testified that after he put Mingo Jack in the lockup he went to the Democratic Primary in Oceanport where he had heard threats being made against Mingo Jack's life by various people. Liebenthal found out the next morning (from his daughter) that Mingo Jack had been hung and went to the lockup to help with the crime scene. Liebenthal said that two clubs had been found inside the lockup and a pick axe was found near the outside of it.

Dr William Beach then spoke about how he had gone to the Herbert house after the assault to tend to Angelina. Dr Beach also examined the body of Mingo Jack and believed that Mingo died as a result of the blow to the head which fractured his right temporal lobe and the forehead over the eye. Dr. Beach did not believe that Mingo was still alive when they had put the noose around his neck, although he did say that the lynching resulted in a broken neck which would have caused immediate death.

Thomas Herbert took the stand next. It was said that many of the jury who were not paying much attention to the trial, suddenly began to take interest when Mr. Herbert was called to testify. On the stand Herbert stated that he had been home all of Friday night, and that both of his sons were at home in bed by ten o'clock. Herbert was sure of this because he was up most of the night tending to his stricken daughter who had been apparently moaning in pain as the effects of the morphine that Dr Beach had given her wore off. The jury and prosecution seemed to believe Mr. Herbert's testimony and while he had perhaps been a prime suspect at first, they did not think it was likely that he had anything to do with the crime. The prosecution now wanted to focus on the story of the men at Allen's saloon in which William Kelly seemed to have volunteered information to Justice Edwards.

Forty six year old James Allen was then called to the stand. He owned Allen's Saloon and was bartending the night of the lynching. Many believe he would have first hand knowledge of all that took place there. However, Mr. Allen claimed he heard nothing and never saw a rope in the hands of William Kelly. He said that he "turned a deaf ear" to the conversation in the bar, and believed that it was not right for a bar owner to listen in on the conversations of his customers. However, he was finally broken down enough by the prosecution to admit that he heard William Kelly say on Saturday morning that "lynching was too good for Mingo Jack." This statement was also confirmed by two other reporters who had been in the saloon at the time. Mr. Kelly, who was still sitting in the courtroom, shouted out that he never said any of those words. Mr. Allen was also able to give the names of the people who were in the saloon the night of the lynching.

Millard Wheeler took the stand and testified that he had seen Mingo Jack Friday afternoon heading in the direction of where the assault took place. Mingo had been near Maps pond cutting ice. He said Mingo was headed in the opposite direction of his house and that he had an axe on his shoulder. Now apparently they had a witness who was able to put Mingo Jack in the vicinity of the assault around the time of when the assault took place. However, later testimony revealed; it might not have been Mingo Jack who Wheeler saw. Mr. Wheeler said he made no threats to take Mingo's life but had heard others make casual threats.

John Maple, Benjamin Bowles, and John Coleman all testified that they had been near the lockup around midnight when they heard gunfire and shouts of "Murder." They did not investigate the matter because they were either too drunk or did not want to get involved with any type of trouble. After this testimony it was getting near the end of the day and the proceedings were adjourned until the following Thursday.

Thursday, March eleventh began the second day of the inquest at Hall's Hotel. Reporters from both Philadelphia and New York packed the courtroom. Once again Coroners Smith and Van Woert were in charge of the case. Counselor James Steen and Prosecutor Swartz also assisted with the inquest. At the start of the day Prosecutor Swartz made an announcement that order and decorum was to be strictly observed in all the proceedings. This was perhaps due to the fact that people had not been taking the case seriously.

The first person called to the stand was William Johnson who lived about a mile from the lockup and had been around the area of Allen's saloon the night after the lynching. He did not have much to contribute to the case and was asked to leave. Jeremiah Thompson was called to the stand next. He was an African American man who had been in Allen's saloon the night of the lynching. He saw the men in the saloon but did not hear them talking about the lynching and did not see a rope or any other type of weapons. However he remarked that the day after the lynching he saw a man by the name of Frank Dangler who had an injury to his nose. While he did not see Mr. Dangler in the saloon that night, others claimed that they had. Some also noticed that Mr. Dangler had a bandage on his hand the day after the lynching. The wounds on Frank Dangler were viewed by the prosecution as being suspicious because they believe it could have been obtained during the lynching. Along with William Kelly, these wounds made Mr. Dangler a prime suspect.

Mr. Thompson also testified that he left Allen's around eight thirty in the evening to talk to Mingo Jack in the lockup. He heard many threats that Mingo would be hung before the night was over, although he could not seem to remember who made those threats. Another African American man by the name of Thomas Riley testified that he was also at Allen's saloon but did not see a rope. In order to advance the case the prosecution believed they would need to put someone on the stand who could testify to seeing the rope in Allen's saloon the night of the lynching. Their wishes would be granted when Edward Johnson and Samuel Howland were to testify.

Edward Johnson was called to the stand and he immediately started giving away incriminating details about what had transpired in Allen's Saloon. Unlike Jeremiah Thompson and Thomas Riley, Johnson had stayed in the saloon until it closed just before midnight. Coincidentally, the closing of Allen's seemed to correspond with the time in which Mingo Jack was lynched. Mr. Johnson said that he did in fact see a rope in Allen's Saloon and that William Kelly had hold of the rope. Johnson said there was no talk of Mingo Jack in the saloon. As Mr. Johnson was walking home he heard screams of "murder" coming from the direction of the lockup. He was on the railroad tracks only about fifty yards from the lockup but said he could not see over there because it was too dark. He got home at twenty after twelve and went to bed for the night.

This testimony gave the prosecution the evidence they needed in order to continue to pursue the growing theory that the many of the lynchers had been drinking in Allen's Saloon prior to the crime. However, there still remained the question of exactly who was involved. Certainly William Kelly seemed to be a prime suspect, however there were obviously more people responsible.

Allen's Saloon as it appears today.
The original building is still standing.

After Mr. Johnson's testimony a number of other witnesses were called to the stand and testified to being in Allen's on Friday night but having not really seen much of anything. Samuel Howland was then called to the stand. He was a laborer in Eatontown and had also been in Allen's Saloon the night of the lynching. At first Howland was very reluctant to say much; however after being further pressed on the issue of a possible rope in Allen's, Howland stated that in fact there was a rope there. He said that William Kelly had it in his hands and that he even tied a knot in the rope. When asked by assistant prosecutor Swartz if there was any conversation about Mingo Jack, he claimed there was not. Howland was also asked if anyone else had the rope in their hands, but Howland could not seem to remember. Howland also claims that he saw Frank Dangler in there but was not sure if Dangler had any visible wounds to his face or hand at the time. A number of times Prosecutor Swartz had to remind Mr. Howland that he did not need to make any statements that would incriminate himself when it came to the subject of the rope in Allen's Saloon. Mr. Howland claimed he stayed in Allen's until it closed around midnight, and did not see anyone heading towards the lockup. Howland testified that he headed straight home and did not hear any pistol shots or cries of murder. In regards to Mr. Howland's testimony, a paper would later say " For pure unadulterated lying, Howland could not be beaten".

The last two witnesses of the day who were called was a couple that lived only one hundred fifty yards from the lockup. They were able to shine some light on what could have possibly taken place at the lockup the night of the lynching. An African American couple named William and Sarah Bedford testified that they went to bed between nine and ten that evening but were awakened by the sound of footsteps and voices near the lockup at around midnight. They both heard pistol shots and what sounded like banging noises. They then said they heard cries of "murder" at least six times. Eventually the cries stopped and then they just heard moaning. Mr. Bedford heard some men talking and he believed they sounded drunk. Bedford looked out towards the lockup but only saw darkness. He claims the men left in a wagon and headed south back into the center of town. Both Mr. and Mrs. Bedford were aware that Mingo Jack was in the lockup and that he was probably being killed but they were afraid to go outside because they thought the crowd of people could turn their rage on them. They claimed that the entire ordeal lasted nearly an hour. After the Bedford's testimony concluded, the inquest was adjourned for the day. The third day of the inquest was scheduled for Monday March fifteenth.

The New York Times ran a story the following day that said the second day of the inquest had been a success. They believed that people were now taking the case much more seriously and that the second day had produced better results then the first. Apparently some of the men who had taken a vow of secrecy regarding the lynching had now broken down and said things they should not have, assuming they were referring to Samuel Howland and Edward Johnson.

Apparently there was also a "snitch" within the group of lynchers who might be willing to "tell all that happened" in exchange for immunity. However, *The Monmouth Democrat* painted a much different picture of the case. They said that the inquest was a complete farce and believed the people who murdered Mingo Jack were going to get away with it. *The Monmouth Democrat* expressed the opinion that much of the witnesses were lying on the stand and that the prosecution was not doing their job in getting the truth from anyone.

The third day of the inquest began at Hall's Hotel on Monday March fifteenth, 1886 as scheduled. The first person called to the stand was James Nafew. Mr. Nafew was the town's druggist. He testified that Frank Dangler had gone to see the druggist on Sunday morning about the wounds he had sustained. Mr. Nafew believed that Mr. Dangler had a broken thumb and a bruised nose. Narfew believed it was from a fall that Mr. Dangler had while he was drunk. Mr. Narfew bandaged up Dangler's hand and sent him on his way.

A tinsmith named Henry Pelt was called to the stand next. He had been in the area of Allen's the night of the lynching but did not really add much to the case other than he had seen Constable Liebenthal come into the barber shop and mention the lynching. Once Pelt finished giving his testimony he was excused from the bench.

Henry Bennet then took the stand and testified that he had been in Allen's saloon on Saturday afternoon when

William Kelly came in and stated "that little piece of rope we had here last night is going to get us all at Freehold (the jail there)." When asked about Frank Dangler, Bennet claimed that no mention was made of Dangler and that Dangler was not in the bar at that time.

During the afternoon break in the inquest, Coroner Van Woert retook the testimony of Angelina Herbert in private. This was done because they did not want her testimony to contaminate the testimony of other witnesses or vice versa. When the inquest came back into session it was announced that her testimony had been taken and that the testimony should have no bearing on the case at the moment.

George Herbert, who was the brother of Angelina, took the stand and described what he had done when he found out that his sister had been assaulted. He testified that he was at home the entire night of the lynching. Both a pick axe and a gun were shown to him and he said that he had never seen either of the weapons before. He was then allowed to leave the stand.

Charles Boice was next called to the stand. He claimed he had been at home Friday night by five o'clock and that he rode down to the lockup at around eight o'clock with Frank Dangler to see Mingo Jack's body. During the car ride Boyce claimed that no mention of the lynching was brought up. Boyce also testified that Frank Dangler had said that he received the injury to his face and hands from a fall outside of the Oceanport Primary. This statement was considered very suspicious for a couple of reasons. In other testimony people claimed that Mr. Dangler got the injury outside Allen's from a fall. Some also claimed that they saw Mr. Dangler in Allen's the night of the lynching, after the Oceanport primary, and he did not have any injury. This inconsistency did not paint Mr. Dangler in a favorable light.

The most important witness of the day was the Editor of *The Eatontown Advisor*, Jacob Coffin. As stated in his editorial that he wrote for *The Eatontown Advisor*, Coffin believed that Mingo Jack got what he deserved and that the inquest should be stopped. Coffin further went on to say that he wished Mingo Jack had lived in the southern United States where he felt the situation would have been dealt with much differently. Coffin testified that Constable Liebenthal had spoken with him after he put Mingo Jack in the lockup. The Constable apparently stated that he believed Mingo Jack would be lynched before morning.

This testimony made it appear as though the Constable was guilty of negligence for not protecting his prisoner. This was the same idea that The Monmouth Democrat had stated only a few days earlier. If the Constable knew Mingo Jack would be lynched, why did he leave him in the unguarded lockup overnight?

Mr. Coffin went on to say that he was at home the night of the lynching which was located about one eight of a mile from the lockup. Coffin testified that even with the windows down he could hear the pistol shots and the cries of murder, but did not think to notify anyone about it because he believed that Mingo was getting what he deserved. Coffin was grilled about his article and was asked if he believed it condoned mob violence. Mr. Coffin believed that the article was a good representation of the position that most of the people in Eatontown had but did not mean for it to be against the law or in contempt of court. The third day of the inquest was then adjourned and it was set to resume on the following Monday.

During the third day of the trial an incident happened in Hall's Hotel that was not widely reported by the newspapers for obvious reasons, but showed just how much of a joke the inquest truly was. One of the jurors, Thomas White, had become extremely drunk and began acting inappropriately. Somehow he managed to pick up the torn hat that was found in the lockup and started placing it on the heads of the other jury members. Then in another disgraceful act, he picked up the rope that was used to lynch Mingo Jack and began to try and lasso people with it in a joking way. Everyone in the courtroom was horrified by what White was doing but tried to ignore him in order to not make it any worse than it already was. Coroner Van Woert was asked if the inquest should be postponed until Mr. White could be brought under control, but Van Woert refused saying that he wanted to proceed. Mr. White was eventually calmed down and the inquest continued. As stated previously, none of the local papers wanted to report on this issue because they knew it would cause uproar. It took *The New York Times* to actually bring the story to light.

Chapter 5

A Friendly Enemy

The fourth day of the inquest began on Monday March twenty second 1886. Immediately there was a change in the atmosphere inside the courtroom. The inquest took on a more serious tone. Many people attribute this to the fact the Constable Charles Strong was now present in the courtroom. The presence of the Constable seemed to keep people under control for fear of possible arrest. The change could also be contributed to the incident that had occurred during the third day of the inquest when the drunken juror used evidence in a joking manner.

The morning session of the trial was primarily devoted to finding out information about twenty five year old Joseph Anderson who had been accused of assaulting Mingo Jack a few years earlier. Anderson had been seen drinking in Allen's the night of the lynching by quite a number of people and then mysteriously vanished the day after the crime occurred.

The first person called to the stand that day was Byron VanBernschoten. There was an attempt made by Prosecutor Swartz to obtain information about two men from Asbury Park who apparently took part in the lynching. It was claimed that one of those two men had been stabbed by Mingo Jack in the lockup as he was fighting for his life. Mr. VanBenscoten declared he had no idea what the prosecutor was talking about. He refused to say that Joseph Anderson had been the first person inside the lockup the night of the lynching. There had been a rumor that Mr. VanBerschoten had told someone that this was the case.

Burr Badgeley, a ticket agent for the New Jersey Shore Railroad, was next to testify. He stated that he had not sold Joseph Anderson a ticket nor had he seen him board a train the day after the lynching. Why the prosecutors would think he would have been the one who sold Mr. Anderson a ticket on a train is anyone's guess.

Mrs. Thomas Anderson, mother of Joseph Anderson, and her daughter Henrietta, were next called to the stand. They asserted that Joseph lived in New York but happened to be home the night of the lynching. They emphasized that Joseph was home in bed by eleven in the evening and that he did not have any blood on his clothes or any marks on his hands and face.

Charles Roswell, who was an Oceanport bartender, was next to testify. Roswell testified that he saw Frank Dangler the night of the lynching and that he did not have any marks on his face. Roswell was apparently at the Oceanport Primary the night of the lynching with Frank Dangler, Constable Liebenthal, and various other people. Roswell heard the Constable say that he would not be surprised if Mingo Jack was dead before the night was over. This, of course, was more damning testimony against the Constable showing that he knew a crime was to take place and did not protect the prisoner. Focusing in on this testimony, Dr Beach was recalled to the stand. He had also been at the Oceanport Primary but could not recall if Constable Liebenthal had made such statements or not.

One of the last witnesses called for the day was George Sickels. He was a young man who worked on his families' farm in Shrewsbury about a mile and a half from the lockup. The Sickels family owned a large amount of land in Shrewsbury and the present day Sickles Park is named after them. Mr. Sickels testified that he had also been drinking in Allen's Saloon the night of the lynching and stayed until it closed around midnight. Apparently after the saloon closed, Sickels walked along the train tracks with a lantern that he had purchased around nine that night. He was with Edward Johnson and apparently both of them heard the pistol shots and the cries of murder. Sickels said he could not see what was going on at the lockup despite only being about twenty yards away. Mr. Johnson apparently turned to Sickels and said, "the boys will torment old Jack half to death tonight." Sickels testified that he did not arrive home until about quarter pass one. Mr. Sickles testimony was very suspicious in a few regards. Why would he suddenly purchase a lantern a few hours before the lynching was to take place? How could he have been in Allen's until midnight, walk near the lockup and have apparently not seen anything? Most interesting about his testimony was that it took him nearly an hour and a half to walk a mile and a half. The average person can generally walk about four miles in an hour and a half, so why did it take Mr. Sickels so long to get home if he did not stop somewhere along the way? This testimony made him a prime suspect in the eyes of the prosecution. A few other people were called to testify about the statements made by Constable Liebenthal, however they were irrelevant and the inquest was adjourned until Friday March 26th.

On Tuesday morning, twenty-third, in a stunning turn of events, Constable Liebenthal was arrested at Hall's Hotel for not protecting Mingo Jack. The charge was officially deemed to be manslaughter. The arrest warrant was executed by Constable Charles Strong of Colts Neck and insured by Justice Lawrence of Freehold. The charge was most likely based on the witness testimony that Constable Liebenthal believed Mingo Jack would be killed and did nothing to stop the murder. The Constable was shocked that he was being arrested but was willing to go to the Freehold jail to take care of the matter. No sooner did he arrive at the jail, than Jacob Shutts of Shrewsbury and butcher Abel Coleman of Eatontown were there to post the $5000 bail ($115,000 in today's dollars) in order for him to be released. By evening the Constable was resting comfortably back at home.

The arrest of the Constable was not well received by the people of Eatontown. They believed the matter had gone too far and that arresting the Constable was unnecessary. Many people in the town liked Constable Liebenthal and believed that he was a very fair minded man. The arrest also caused many of the prime suspects that were in Allen's the night of the lynching to become worried. They believed that it would not be long before warrants were issued for their arrests. Counselor Steen believed that the arrest of the Constable was necessary but also stated that he would not be "pushed too hard." Coroner's Van Woert and Smith were not happy at all with the arrest occurring before the end of the inquest. They believed the charges would only serve to make the public side with the lynchers and only make their case more difficult.

On Friday March twenty seventh, the fifth day of the inquest began. Prosecutor Swartz, along with Coroners Van Woert and Smith, once again presided. The first order of business was a request by the prosecution to remove Constable Liebenthal from the case. Prosecutor Smith stood up and said, "Mr Liebenthal, I think your services will no longer be needed in the case. You are a prisoner at the instance of the prosecution; therefore I think you are disqualified from serving further on this inquest." The Constable was shocked by this request and became angry.

He believed that he would lose money if he was removed. The Constable exclaimed that he would never be convicted of any wrongdoing and appealed to the coroners to reverse the decision made by prosecutor Swartz. However, both coroners also agreed that it would be best if he was removed. Constable Liebenthal reluctantly stepped down and was replaced by Constable Strong.

The first witness called for the day was William Reid who was the employer of George Sickles. Mr. Reid was the person who, along with Mr. Sickles, had purchased the lantern the night of the lynching and the prosecution hoped he could provide more insight into the events of the night in question. Mr. Reid stated that he had spoken with Mr. Sickels about splitting the cost of a lantern. Apparently the reason they wanted to purchase one was because Mr. Sickels had accidently broken Mr. Reid's the night before. However, the prosecution put forth the point that it had been stated that Mr. Reid's lantern had been broken for nearly three weeks. It still seemed very suspicious that Mr. Sickles had a sudden need to buy a lantern on the night of the lynching. Joseph Johnson, who was a storekeeper in Eatontown then stepped forward and said that he had sold Mr. Sickles the lantern on the night of the lynching for one dollar.

Samuel Armock was called to the stand next. He was a dealer of kindling wood and kept his horse at the saw mill which was only one hundred and fifty yards from the lockup. Mr. Armonk testified that he had been at the lockup the morning after the lynching and had seen a crowbar near the lockup. Armock asked Samuel Billings if the crowbar had belonged to him and Mr. Billings believed that it had. However, the crowbar in question disappeared before it was collected as evidence. It is believed that this could have been the crowbar used to break open the jail.

Garret Morton was called to the stand and testified that he had also been at the lockup the morning after the lynching. Initially Mr. Morton had claimed that William Kelly had made several statements about the rope in Allen's saloon being used in the lynching. However, once Mr. Morton was put on the stand, he denied ever making such statements. The prosecution continued to try and push him, but they were unsuccessful.

The afternoon session began with an attempt by the prosecution to prove that Mingo Jack was innocent. Here is a discrepancy of some of the testimony that Angelina had given in private to the prosecution the day before because it has some bearing on the subsequent testimony. Keep in mind what she said was only known to the prosecution at the time because they did not want to prejudice the testimony that had yet to be given. Much of what Angelina testified to was very similar to what *The Red Bank Registry* had retrieved from her and printed in their paper a few days after the attack. However, there were a few other details that Angelina had included such as the description of Mingo Jack's clothes.

Angelina testified that Mingo Jack was wearing "blue Dunham overalls and a coat with brass buttons; the brass buttons might have been half an inch large. He had on a dirty brown hat; a very small derby." The prosecution hoped that they could use this testimony to prove Mingo Jack innocent by bringing forward witnesses who could verify he was not wearing the clothes that Angelina claimed he was wearing. She also stated that she had been totally conscious during the entire attack and well aware of her surroundings. Previously she stated that she had lost consciousness.

The first witness called in the afternoon was Jackson Brown. His house was where Angelina was headed the day she was attacked. Mr. Brown had been working at Maps Saw Mill on the afternoon of the attack. Just before four that afternoon, Brown claimed he saw Mingo Jack head over the Maps Pond Bridge with an axe on his shoulder, in the direction of where Miss Herbert had been seen earlier. However, Mr. Brown could not recall the clothes Mingo had on. Mr. Brown also testified that he saw another African American man by the name of Gilbert Polhemus cross over the same bridge on Poplar Road a few minutes after Mingo did. The prosecution was interested to find out if Mr. Polhemus had seen anything that day and he was called to the stand. Polhemus stated that he had not seen either Miss Herbert or Mingo Jack on the day in question, but remembered being in the area around the time of the attack. He testified that he was cutting wood near the Whale Pond Bridge and did in fact have an axe on his shoulders. Mr Polhemus said that he was wearing yellow overalls and a blue coat on the day in question. The prosecution did not view Mr. Polhemus as a suspect in the attack simply because yellow overalls would have been highly distinguishable. However Mr. Polhemus made an unusual statement to a man by the name of Lawrence Prince. Polhemus said that he believed that if Angelina Herbert had been killed instead of just raped, that he would have been the prime suspect.

Edward Williams was called to the stand next. He was a farmer in Shrewsbury and on the day of the lynching had been heading south on Poplar Road towards Ocean Township around one on the afternoon of the attack on Miss Herbert. He was carting marl, which was a rich soil that gave the current town of Marlboro, New Jersey it's name. Mr. Williams noticed Mingo Jack on the side of the road heading south. Williams picked Mingo up and took him about a mile south to Jim Crummel's house. Williams claimed that Mingo was on his way there to chop wood for the day and had an axe with him. Unfortunately he could not remember what Mingo Jack was wearing. It is interesting to note that both Mingo Jack and Gilbert Polhemus had an axe with them on the day of the attack; however Miss Herbert testified that she was positive her attacker did not have an axe with him. It is also possible that Mr. Brown had not even seen Mingo Jack, but rather Gilbert Polhemus crossing over the Maps Pond drawbridge, since the man was more then fifty yards away. On the first day of the inquest Millard Wheeler also testified to seeing a man with an axe and had assumed it was Mingo Jack.

At this point during the inquest Mingo Jack's clothes that he was wearing when he was lynched were brought into the courtroom. Merritt Leach, a butcher in Eatontown, was called to the stand next. Over the course of five years he had worked on and off with Mingo Jack doing various odd jobs. Mr. Leach claimed that Mingo had helped him move into his house in Long Branch about six months prior. Leach was asked if he had ever seen Mingo Jack wear a derby hat. To the shock of the prosecution, he asserted he had never seen Mingo Jack with a derby hat. Leach testified that Mingo usually wore either a jockey hat or a "wide awake" cap. Neither of these hats look anything like a derby hat.

Mingo Jack's thirty eight year old daughter, Henrietta Johnson, was then called to the stand. She also stated that Mingo Jack had never worn a derby hat and had never owned any blue Durham overalls. When showed the clothes that Mingo was lynched in she said that those clothes were what he usually wore. She said Mingo never changed clothes in the middle of the day and the ones that were being shown in the courtroom were the clothes he had on the morning he left the house to go cut wood at Jim Crummel's house. Of course the clothes that were shown looked absolutely nothing like the ones that Miss Herbert had testified that he attacker wore. The prosecution began to truly believe that Mingo Jack was indeed innocent of the crime committed; however they had nothing more than circumstantial evidence to go on. After the testimony of Miss Johnson, the inquest was adjourned until Tuesday March thirtieth.

After the inquest had been adjourned a number of the jury members stayed behind and were asked to be removed from the case. They believed that the inquest had gone on exceptionally long and that they had better things to do than continue to serve. A shouting match between the jurors and the coroners ensued and the jurors were told that if they did not continue to serve for the remainder of the trial, they would be held in contempt of court and severely punished. The jurors said nothing and simply left the hotel; feeling defeated in their efforts to be released. Of course the jury members were not the only ones who were getting tired of the prosecution. Many threatening letters had begun to arrive at their offices to tell them to stop the inquest. One of these letters to Prosecutor John Swartz is printed below; it stands as an example of how some people believe that Mingo had gotten what he deserved.

"John W. Swartz:

Hearken to the call of a friendly voice unto thee who art in everlasting danger. Hearken, I say, for the day of vengeance is nights at hand, when thou will fall 'neath the touch of a glittering blade.

Cease thy course in the Mingo Jack matter; or afore long days, when the golden sun rises in the eastern sky; it will rise to shine upon the lifeless body of John W. Swartz. Beware I say and heed this timely warning or thou will cry when it is too late.

-A friendly enemy"

While the inquest was taking place, the war between Monmouth County's newspapers continued. *The Asbury Park Press* published a story about two African American men committing sexual assault against a white woman in Eatontown a year earlier. The men were convicted of a small crime and sentenced to three months in jail. Since both men were poor, being sent to jail where they were given shelter and fed was actually a reward and not a punishment. The people of Eatontown had not been happy with this decision and *The Asbury Park Press* believed that this was one of the reasons the locals had murdered Mingo Jack.

Major James Yard, who was an editor of *The Monmouth Democrat*, read this story and became angry because he believed *The Asbury Park Press* was again trying to justify the murder. He wrote in his column that no such assault had actually taken place in Eatontown, but that it had instead taken place in South Jersey. He stated that the two men who were guilty of the crime did not get just three months in jail, but a few years. He said that jail was not a reward for them but a punishment and he believed

The Asbury Park Press was irresponsible in posting an incorrect story.

The Red Bank Registry saw an opportunity to make *The Monmouth Democrat* look foolish. They pulled up archives from the previous year where *The Monmouth Democrat* had indeed reported on the story of the rape in Eatontown and that it had occurred just as *The Asbury Park* Press had described it. *The Red Bank Registry* then said that the Editor of *The Monmouth Democrat* should be removed for his irresponsibility. What all three papers were guilty of was straying from the story at hand. Instead of focusing on the murder of Mingo Jack, they used another story to go to war with each other.

On Tuesday March thirtieth 1886 the sixth day of the inquest began. Despite a severe rainstorm that was taking place, many people managed to make it into Hall's Hotel. Due to the pressures the prosecution had received to end the inquest, this would be the last day of testimony and a verdict by the jury would be delivered at the day's conclusion.

Peter Hall, owner of Halls' Hotel, was recalled to the stand. He was asked about some statements he might have made about lynching Mingo Jack. Hall denied making such statements. He was also questioned about writing some letters to Freehold about the lynching. Mr. Hall also denied writing such letters. The prosecution realized they were not going to get much more from Mr. Hall and excused him from the bench.

The next person to be called to the stand was James Roswell. He worked in various hotels in the area and lived about three and a half miles south of Eatontown. Roswell was asked if he had been in Allen's the night of the lynching and Roswell claimed he had not been there. Prosecutor Swartz became annoyed with Mr. Roswell because he believed Roswell was lying. Swartz said that three other men had all sworn that they had seen Roswell at Allen's on the night of the lynching and that he had a rope in his hands. Mr. Roswell stuck to his story though and said all the men were lying.

The Prosecution noticed Roswell had red stains on his boots and wanted to know what caused the stains. Mr. Roswell said he was not sure but was more than willing to pass the boots around to the jury so that they could make up their minds. Roswell finally said that he believed it was red paint and not blood (which had been suggested). However, Mr. Roswell did finally admit that he was drinking at Hall's Hotel on the night of the lynching and had apparently asked for some "rye whiskey" to take with him as he left.

William Kelly was recalled to the stand next, but he did not appear. Constable Liebenthal was asked if he knew anything about Mr. Kelly's whereabouts. The Constable stated that he had served a subpoena on Kelly and that he should be there. Everyone in the room was questioned and no one seemed to have any idea where Mr. Kelly was. County Clerk Patterson spoke up and said that he had seen Kelly in Freehold the previous day.

Prosecutor Swartz began to realize that Mr. Kelly most likely had fled the area in order to avoid having to testify. His first time on the stand at the beginning of the inquest was anything short of a disaster and many believed he was a prime suspect in the lynching.

Eventually a man who worked for the associated press by the name of J. Towley Crane stood up and stated that he had been with Mr. Kelly the previous day. They had taken the train together to Red Bank and then got on a ferry that went to New York City. Mr. Crane stated that while on the ferry Mr. Kelly had told him that there was a rope in Allen's saloon and that he had tied a knot in it and put it around a man's neck to "see how it worked." But according to Mr. Crane, William Kelly denied having taken any part in the lynching of Mingo Jack. Crane claimed that Mr. Kelly was in NYC to see Kelly's sister and when they parted ways he said he would be back in Eatontown the following day to testify. But obviously Mr. Kelly never showed up for the final day of the inquest.

Catherine Crummell was called to the witness stand. She was the wife of Jim Crummell. She stated that on the day of the assault Mingo Jack had been at her home cutting wood. She believed he had arrived at eight in the morning and worked until nearly three that afternoon. Mingo Jack's clothes were shown to her and she testified that they were the same clothes he had on the day he was at her house. She also stated that she had never seen Mingo in blue Dunham overalls or wearing a derby hat.

Before the jury was sent to deliberate the charges, Prosecutor Swartz addressed the courtroom. He gave a summary of the case and asked the jury to focus on a few important points. He claimed that based on testimony, Tom Little, Edward Johnson, and George Sickles were near the lockup around the time the lynching took place. He stated that a lot of suspicious activity took place in Allen's Saloon on the night of the lynching and that William Kelly had admitted that there had been a rope which people were tying knots in at the saloon. Swartz mentioned that both Joseph Anderson and William Kelly had fled the area after the lynching at that Joseph Anderson had been accused of assault on Mingo Jack in the past. He also brought up the fact that Frank Dangler had suspicious wounds on his face the following day. The Prosecutor said he swore an oath to uphold the law and that it was his duty to hold the inquest despite the protests to stop it. He was disappointed that he did not fully have the support of the Eatontown people during that inquest. Swartz ended with the comment that regardless of what the verdict was, all of the men he mentioned would likely be arrested and charged with the crime of lynching Mingo Jack.

At three fifteen that afternoon Officer Strong sent the jury into a secluded room and instructed them to remain until they had reached a verdict. Nearly two hours later the jury returned and announced their verdict. They stated that Mingo Jack had been "willfully murdered at the Eatontown lock-up." However they went onto add that the crime had been committed by "some person or persons unknown". They also said that the editor of *The Eatontown advisor*, Jacob Coffin, would receive "a severe rebuke and censure" for condoning mob violence. A few of the people in the courtroom voiced their displeasure over the verdict. Some believed that no censure was needed and that Mingo Jack had gotten what he deserved. However, for the most part the verdict was not a shock based on the testimony that had been given.

As the Prosecutor had promised the men mentioned began to be arrested. Between April second and April fifth Constable Strong arrested Edward H. Johnson, Frank Dangler, William Kelly, Joseph Anderson, Tom Little, and George Sickles. All the men were charged in the lynching of Mingo Jack. As soon as the arrests occurred, their friends were at the Freehold jail to bond them out. Shrewsbury resident and owner of the historic Allen House, Joseph Allen bailed out Frank Dangler. He claimed he was worth the $4,000 that was needed to get Mr. Dangler out of prison. Joseph and William Buck of Freehold came to the aid of George Sickles. Sickles was released after they posted the $4,000 bail. The rest of the men soon had friends and family compile money in order for them to get bonded out. All the men indicted for the crime hired forty four year old Eatontown attorney Henry Clayton to defend them in the upcoming criminal case.

Chapter 6

They All Took Their Oaths

On Tuesday, April fourteenth there was a session held by the Freeholders in order to discuss payment of the bills incurred during the inquest. When it came to county taxpayer dollars, the Freeholders wanted to make sure they were not getting ripped off. The first bill submitted was for compensation of the witnesses, jury, and coroners. It was decided that they were due their promised compensation. However, there was some discussion about whether or not the jury should receive additional money because the inquest was exceptionally long. There was a law that stated each jury member could receive additional money for a long inquest. This request was approved, but it was sent back to the petitioners by Constable Conover in order to be written to fit the law.

The next bill paid was for Constable Liebenthall's services in the inquest. The bill was initially submitted for nineteen dollars; however the Freeholders reduced it to twelve dollars and approved it for payment. There was also a bill put on the table to pay for the burial of Mingo Jack in a pauper's grave. The bill for the burial came to a total of fifteen dollars. The Freeholders initially did not believe it was their responsibility to pay for the burial, but then later approved it. The next bill put forth was for the use of Hall's Hotel. Peter Hall wanted to be compensated one hundred and five dollars for use of the room. Many of the Freeholders believed the cost was ridiculous. Mr. Eaton came to Mr. Hall's defense and said that the room had sustained damage to it during the inquest that would cost nearly fifty dollars to repair. However, as stated earlier, it was said that Mr. Hall made so much money off the sale of alcohol that it more then made up for the damages. Mr. Hall's bill was reduced to seventy dollars and approved for payment.

Various other bills were put forth for the doctors, prosecution, and law enforcement. Most of them were paid, some were reduced. When all was said and done the total cost of the ordeal came to nearly $500 ($12,000 in today's money). Many of the taxpayers were outraged by what they believed were excessive bills. Both *The Red Bank Registry* and *The Monmouth Democrat* went back and forth with what bills should or should not have been paid. Even months after the attack, the papers would still post editorials about how the Mingo Jack bills were an excessive waste of taxpayer money. However there were no changes in the payments and the issue eventually died down.

On Saturday April eleventh a hearing was held in Trenton to decide if there was enough evidence to bring indictments against the men charged with the lynching of Mingo Jack. The prosecution consisted of Prosecutor Haight, Assistant Prosecutor Swartz, and Counselor Steen, with Judge Edward Scudder presiding over the hearing. It was the Prosecution's position that the men should not be allowed to go free on bail because they had been charged with a capital crime. The prosecution then submitted the testimony from the witnesses at the inquest and requested that copies of telegrams from Western Union be obtained. These telegrams were communication between all the suspects involved in the case. The prosecution believed they contained information regarding the lynching; however Judge Scudder saw them as private communications. E.J Brady, a representative from Western Union, was told to send the telegrams to the Judge and he would decide if they contained any relevant information. If not the judge planned to have them destroyed.

Testimony in the case continued without the Western Union telegrams. A number of witnesses were called to testify against the men accused and their part in the lynching. A private detective named Theodore Wandell was called to the stand. Mr. Wandell had made his way into the town by posing as an owner of a racing stable. He testified that during the inquest Edward Johnson told him that he and George Sickles had to swear to each other to tell the same stories on the stand about what happened the night of the lynching. Mr. Wandell made a remark to Mr. Johnson that there were too many people involved in the lynching and that someone would eventually crack. Mr. Johnson replied, "No they won't; they all took their oaths."

During the hearing a number of other people were called to the stand, they were, Constable Roswell, Constable Strong, William Allen, Thomas Muckenback, Henry Johnson, Charles Maps, and Samuel Maps. Mr Muckenback was Frank Dangler's brother in-law and Henry Johnson was the brother of Edward Johnson. Both men were called in as character witnesses. Other than Mr. Wandell's testimony, not much was really elicited from any of these witnesses that had not already been learned from the testimony at the inquest. Judge Scudder adjourned the hearing and made the decision that all the men would be allowed to remain free on bail.

On Sunday April ninetieth there was another twist in the case. Constable Strong arrested thirty four year old William Snedeker at the Wolf Hill Tollhouse in Oceanport. The warrant had been issued by Judge Lawrence and the charge was for killing Mingo Jack. Up until this point Mr. Snedeker's name had not been mentioned and it was unclear what his connection to the case was. *The New York Times* ran an article about Mr. Snedeker's arrest. *The Times* believed that he was the informant who was willing to break his oath and tell the court what had happened.

They believed this was the only explanation for him not being involved with the inquest.

Mr. Snedeker hired Mr. Mcdermott and Mr. Throckmorton to defend him against the charges. They filed a writ of habeas corpus with Judge Scudder, with it being returnable April twenty second. The bail hearing for William Snedeker was held on April twenty second at ten thirty in the morning. Prosecutor Swartz represented the State and said that Mr. Snedeker had been arrested because he had confessed to Constable Roswell that he had been involved in the lynching of Mingo Jack.

The Constable was called to the stand and according to him, Mr. Snedeker stated "we hung Mingo Jack; Tom Little put the rope around his neck and I helped pull him up; my God, how he begged and prayed." The Constable went onto say that he saw Mr. Snedeker the next morning at Dan White's Hotel in Oceanport and the first words out of Mr. Snedeker's mouth were, "Charlie, we killed the nigger." The Constable said that Mr. Snedeker looked terrible and it appeared as though he may have been drinking the night before. The Constable said it was possible that Snedeker could have still been drunk that morning as well. Upon cross examination from the defense, Constable Roswell admitted that Mr. Snedeker liked to tell stories and brag about things that did not take place while Snedeker was drunk. The defense surmised that Mr. Snedeker admitting to the murder of Mingo Jack was simply another one of his stories.

Mr. Shade Tallman was called to the stand next and he basically corroborated the testimony of Constable Roswell. According to his testimony, he was in Dan White's Hotel the morning after the lynching when Mr. Snedeker came in and testified that he had helped kill Mingo Jack.

A number of witnesses then testified in defense of Mr. Snedeker. Joseph Manning and James Megill both testified that they had been at the Primary with Mr. Snedeker the night of the lynching. They claimed that Mr. Snedeker got very drunk at the Primary and that they stayed there until quarter passed midnight. The men then walked to the railroad crossing in Eatontown where Mr. Snedeker was left with Tom Little at about ten minutes before one in the morning. This information did not fit the timeline of when Mingo Jack was murdered, which was said to have taken place just after midnight. It is possible that the men were covering for Mr. Snedeker, were mistaken of the time, or that Tom Little and William Snedeker had nothing to do with the lynching.

Milford Jeffries testified that he was with Mr. Snedeker around one in the morning and that Snedeker was very drunk. Jefferies claimed that both of them went back to his house and went to bed soon after. Mr. Jeffries claimed that he left the house at around seven in the morning and that Mr. Snedeker was still fast asleep.

A stage driver by the name of Joseph Chance contradicted Mr. Jeffries testimony. He claimed that Mr.

Snedeker was at White's Hotel in Oceanport at seven in the morning and was "beastly drunk".

Martin Ferns took the stand and testified that Snedeker was with Tom Little and that Mr. Ferns walked with them back to his house. Judge Scudder set bail at $3,000 for Mr. Snedeker and said that he should be held for the Grand Jury. The bond was signed by farmers Daniel White and Garrett Conover and Mr. Snedeker was allowed to be released on bail.

With the arrest of these men to face the Grand Jury it appeared that justice was moving forward in the case. *The Monmouth Democrat* and *Red Bank Registry* both posted stories that justice would soon be had in the Mingo Jack lynching. However, for whatever reason, the grand jury decided not to pursue charges on any of the men accused of being involved in the lynching. It is unknown exactly why this happened; perhaps it was due to a lack of evidence. The story of their vindication went largely unreported in the papers.

By this time the public seemed to be ready to move on with their lives and forget about what had happened to Angelina Herbert and Mingo Jack despite so many unanswered questions. Little did they know that in the years to come there would be reminders of the case and of the possibility that Mingo Jack was innocent after all.

Chapter 7

Voluntary Confession

In April 1888, less than two years after the murder of Mingo Jack, another African American male, Richard Kearny confessed to the assault against Angelina Herbert. This came as a shock to many people in the county. Mr. Kearny was already set to be hung on July 18, 1888 for the murder of Mrs. Margaret Purcell in Elberon. A short confession was written up which was signed by Mr. Kearny. The confession is as follows:

I, Richard Kearney, late of Long Branch, New Jersey, convicted of murder in the first degree of Margaret Purcell, and under the sentence of death.......do make the following full, free, and voluntary confession, without any hope of respite, new trial, or pardon.

In March, 1886 I worked for Mr. William Henderson at Cedar Avenue, West Long Branch, NJ. I had been at work for him a year then. I knew Angelina Herbert by sight. I remember hearing of the attempted crime on her person. I know Samuel Johnson, alias "Mingo Jack", being arrested and lynched for that crime; that was in the month of March 1886. I know who committed the crime on her. It was myself, Richard Kearney, who did it. It was about a quarter of a mile from where she lived to the place where I did it in the woods. I first saw her about two hundred yards from the pond coming through the woods, coming from her home and going toward Hoppertown. I had a little stick in my hand, and I touched her on the shoulder and she turned and said, "I thought it was Bob Johnson". I said no. I asked her if she knew Bob Johnson's father. I said Bob Johnson is Mingo Jack's son. She said she did not know him. After the occurrence in the woods, I went back to the pond (Maps Pond) and got load of ice, and then went back home to William Henderson's with a load of ice. When I first saw Miss Herbert, I was on a wagon in the company with .... and .... I got out of the wagon and went after Miss Herbert, and they drove on to the pond. Mingo Jack was not there in the woods when I was there with Miss Herbert, and I did not see him that day.

Once again news reporters descended on the Herbert house to talk with Angelina to get her reaction to this new allegation. They wondered if it could be possible that an innocent man had been murdered. Angelina was apparently not home at the time the reporters showed up, however it is far more likely that she was bedridden due to her tuberculosis which was progressively getting worse. The reporters were met by a not so happy Sarah Herbert who shouted to them that it was without a doubt Mingo Jack who had assaulted her daughter. She went on to add that any mention of the matter to the family would only caused more hardships that they did not need. Her daughter was ailing and she did not want aggressive reporters making her worse.

The news paper's reactions to this confession were interesting and showed each of their biases in the case. *The Red Bank Registry* ran the headline "A humbug confession." They immediately dismissed it as nothing more then a fabrication and attempted to pick apart the confession. They interviewed William Henderson who claimed that Mr. Kearney did not work for him during that time and that there was no ice near where Mr. Kearney had stated there was. They obviously believed that Mr. Kearney would simply say anything to save himself from death.

The Monmouth Democrat ran an assertive headline that said "Mingo Jack is Innocent." They went back and pointed to the evidence that Mingo's clothes did not match the descriptions of Angelina's testimony. They were not one hundred percent sure that it was indeed Mr. Kearney who had committed the crime, but they believed that this was simply more proof that Mingo Jack was indeed innocent. They did not believe it would make much sense for another man to confess to the crime if it was certain beyond a reasonable doubt that Mingo Jack was guilty.

A few days before his execution, Richard Kearney retracted his confession. He said that the only reason he wrote it was because he somehow believed he would be offered clemency from being hung, however this was never the case. Mr. Kearney also stated that he was coerced into giving the confession by the Constable of Red Bank named Frank Patterson after some local gang members had said that Kearney was responsible. Law enforcement was quick to deny that any type of coercion had been given to elicit a confession from Mr. Kearney. Kearney also stated that he believed that he was not responsible for the death of Ms. Purcell despite the fact that he had repeatedly thrown her down a flight of stairs in her house. Either way Mr. Kearny was hung as scheduled in Freehold for the murder of Mrs. Purcell and later buried in Eatontown's White Ridge Cemetery in an unmarked grave.

On May forth 1893 at the age of thirty one, Angelina Herbert died of tuberculosis at her home in Eatontown. It had only been seven years since the attack. Her death made headlines in *The New York Times* and local Monmouth County papers. It was said that she never fully recovered from the assault by Mingo Jack and that it was a contributing factor to her death. After a service at the families' local church Angelina was buried in West Long Branch at the Methodist Church cemetery on Locust avenue. Her grave, as well as the graves of her parents, are unmarked. Her death certificate is on record at the Trenton Hall of records. It confirmed her date of death as well as listing tuberculosis as the cause.

Soon after her death in 1893 there was another twist in the case against Mingo Jack. A Phidelphia reporter by the name of William Beecher noticed Angelina's death notice in *The Asbury Park Press*. Angelina's death notice apparently jogged Mr. Beecher's memory of a story that he had reported on a number of years earlier. This reporter claimed that an African American man by the name of John Miller had confessed to the assault against Angelina in December of 1888. Mr. Miller was on his deathbed dying of typhoid fever when he made the confession. Mr. Miller had apparently been aboard a ship called the Congo. After the assault on Angelina and the lynching of Mingo Jack, Miller apparently fled the Monmouth County area to evade any type of prosecution. Mr Beecher broke this story in the *Philadelphia Sunday Dispatch*, which was the paper he worked for at the time.

Unfortunately, there isn't much else known about John Miller. He does not seem to appear in the census records in the area and no one seemed to recall him. *The Red Bank Registry* was quick to dismiss this story as nonsense, running only a small editorial that mentioned how it was ridiculous that people kept claiming to have committed the assault. *The Monmouth Democrat* did not even mention the confession, perhaps because they had also grown tired of the story or perhaps they felt like they had been embarrassed by the Richard Kearney confession.

Chapter 8

Revenge

In January of 1899 there were efforts made to close the Locust Grove Cemetery where Mingo Jack was buried. The cemetery had been used as a pauper's burial ground for nearly one hundred years and running out of places to bury people. A larger piece of land was bought on Wall Street and became know as White Ridge Cemetery. Many of the bodies in Locust Grove Cemetery were exhumed and reburied in White Ridge. According to *The Red Bank Registry*, Mingo's grave had been marked with a stake and two horse bones. However by the turn of the century both of these had disappeared and his grave could no longer be located.

It is unclear whether or not Mingo Jack's body was ever moved to White Ridge Cemetery. No one seems to know and there are no records on it. Many of the plots were moved, the cemetery was condensed and office buildings today that sit directly across from the area may have once been part of the cemetery. In any case, a few bodies and headstones still remain in Locust Grove Cemetery. For many years it had become overgrown with brush, but recently there have been efforts to clear some of the brush away and restore what is left of the cemetery. In 1999, Joseph Dangler (a relative of Frank Dangler) drew a map indicating where Mingo Jack had been buried in Locust Grove. This map is currently in the possession of the Monmouth County Hall of Records. What is left of the cemetery lies between Wyckoff Road and Highway 35, just behind a Quickchek.

Locust Grove Cemetery as it appears today.
(Photo courtesy of author)

In late May of 1901, Mingo Jack got revenge on one of the men who was perhaps responsible for his murder.

William Kelly was arrested late one night for being drunk in public and put in the Eatontown lockup. This is of course the same spot Mingo Jack had been lynched fifteen years earlier. Mr. Kelly was expected to stay the night there, however after only a few hours in the solitary cell he was getting extremely scared and begged to pay the fine and be released before the night was over. The Constable fined him three dollars and seventy five cents and let him out of the cell. What transpired over the few hours in the lockup is not known. But it is quite ironic that Mingo was able to get revenge from beyond the grave. In fact there had been numerous sightings of his ghost near the lockup, floating over Mill Pond, and near his grave in Locust Grove Cemetery. Of course it could be folklore, but perhaps Mr. Kelly did see Mingo's ghost in the lockup that night.

I personally do not believe that Mingo Jack was responsible for the attack on Angelina Herbert. The main piece of evidence I use for this is the simple fact that his clothes did not match the description of the clothes Miss Herbert testified he wore. With quite a number of witnesses stating that Mingo Jack had never worn the type of clothes that Angelina had described it is doubtful that Mingo Jack committed the crime. Angelina also testified that the attacker asked "Do you know Mingo Jack?" It does not make any sense that an attacker would identify themselves to their victim. Angelina had never been closer to Mingo Jack than about fifty yards (the distance from her house to the road) so it unclear how she could have possibly known it was him. That is more than enough distance from someone to not be able to identify facial features. Perhaps when the attacker mentioned Mingo Jack's name, it made Angelina believe it was him, when it fact it was not. While Angelina Herbert was certain that it was Mingo who had attacked her, she made reference that she "knew him by his clothes". This tends to imply that she really did not know what he looked liked. I don't believe that Angelina would have intentionally accused an innocent man of the crime; I just believe that it was a case of mistaken identity. When Mingo Jack was arrested he was reportedly sitting down and having dinner with his family. If he had just committed an attack, it defies logic that he would be sitting calmly at the dinner table with his family. Although it should also be noted that some accounts say he was not sitting down to dinner but simply "sitting by the fireplace with his coat off".

Richard Kearney was probably not the attacker either. As *The Red Bank Registry* pointed out, his confession was full of holes, and sounded like information he had heard from newspaper accounts of the assault. Also the fact that he recanted his confession and had good reason to lie about it to begin with seems to make it highly suspicious. It is also possible that Mr. Kearney had been coerced into making the confession.

There is not enough information on John Miller to make a presumption of guilt or innocence. There is a chance that he did not even exist. Of course there is just as much of a chance that he was the one responsible. Since very little is known about Miller and over one hundred and twenty years have elapsed, it would be nearly impossible to find any information on him or the confession he made other than what appeared in the local papers just after Angelina Herbert died.

Attempts were made to find the living relatives of William Beecher in hopes that they would know more about the story he had written about John Miller. Unfortunately those efforts proved useless. If any good came from the confessions of John Miller and Richard Kearny it is that they were able to cast more doubt on the belief that Mingo Jack was indeed the attacker. It is quite a shame the Eatontown did not follow up with this case when these new confessions were made.

Many of the people involved in the lynching were obviously in Allen's saloon. It was just across the street from the site of the lynching. Many questionable things occurred there the night of the lynching and the saloon was the main focus of the inquest. The two people who stand out to me as having involvement were Frank Dangler and William Kelly. Mr. Kelly obviously admitted about having the rope that most likely was used to lynch Mingo Jack. He also fled to New York when called to testify which would seen to indicate that he was guilty in some respect. Frank Dangler could not seem to keep his stories straight about how he received the injuries to his hand and face and it seems quite coincidental that he received the injuries on the night of the lynching.

Both Edward Johnson and George Sickels stories did not make much sense either. They were both in Allen's the night of the lynching and just happened to be near the lockup with their newly purchased lantern right around the time of the lynching. Add to that the information that it took George Sickles an extremely long time to walk home from his house. Their stories simply do not add up. William Snedeker and Tom Little were certainly involved with the crime. I believe that the men put on the stand to testify for them lied under oath about being with them around the time of the lynching. I believe they also intentionally exaggerated the time they left Mr. Snedeker to make it seem as though he arrived back in Eatontown nearly an hour after the lynching took place. They must have been aware of the time the lynching took place and simply added an hour to it to make it seem as though both Tom Little and William Snedeker were innocent.

One cannot blame the jury of either the inquest or the trial for making the decisions they did. At the time there simply was no enough evidence to change anyone criminally. If I had been on the jury I most likely would have delivered the same verdict. In the era of substandard laws and very little technology, there simply was not much to work with to prove the men were guilty beyond a reasonable doubt. If there is any good to come out of the lynching of Mingo Jack, it's assurance that something like this would never take place in the twenty first century. DNA evidence from the lockup would have been able to solve both the attack against Miss Herbert and the crime against Mingo very quickly. Although in all likelihood, the crime against Mingo Jack would have never happened today, because prisoners are afforded protection from any type of retaliatory attacks.

Most people today are probably somewhat shocked that this crime did not spark more racial tensions between whites and blacks. There were obviously racial undertones to the case, but many in the African American community just accepted it for what it was. However, I guess there is a reasonable explanation for this. Even though the crime took place forty years after slavery was outlawed in New Jersey, it would still be decades before the civil rights movement began to gain traction. Many in the African American community must have simply accepted the circumstances and did not feel they could speak out against the injustice that had taken place.

Nearly thirty years after Mingo Jack was murdered a strikingly similar case occurred just ten miles from Eatontown. On November 10, 1910 a ten year old girl by the name of Marie Smith was walking home from school in Asbury Park when she vanished. Her body was discovered a few days later in a wooded area off Asbury Avenue. Marie had been beaten, raped, and strangled to death. The prime suspect in the case was an African American man by the name of Thomas Williams who had been seen drinking in the area at the time. Like Mingo Jack, he also had a nickname he was known by; Black Diamond. Black Diamond was arrested for the murder of the girl, and a crowd of lynchers went to the jail to kill him. Many of them even openly bragged that they had been part of the Mingo Jack lynching. However this time things were different, Black Diamond was rushed to a safer jail in Freehold. Unlike the Mingo Jack case, a major investigation took place and it was later determined that Black Diamond had nothing to do with the murder of Marie. A German man by the name of Frank Heideman was ultimately convicted of the crime. However this case shows a similar rush to judgment that was very much evident in the Mingo Jack case. This case also shows that racial undertones were still very much present.

Chapter 9

Out Of Sight, Out Of Mind.

As the decades went by the story of Mingo Jack's murder and the assault on Angelina Herbert began to be forgotten, until it almost totally faded from memory. Today there are very few Monmouth County residents who know the story happened. The areas around Eatontown also began to change. The once desolate Poplar Road where Mingo Jack and the Herberts lived slowly became more active. Today it is known as Highway 35 and is one of the busiest highways in the county. Both the Herbert and Johnson families stayed in Eatontown for the remainder of their lives. When they passed away the houses were demolished and retail buildings were eventually put up in their place. Today there is a Dunkin Donuts Plaza at the spot where Mingo Jack use to live and a small wooded park sits on the hill where the Herbert house was located, just across from the Red Lobster restaurant. Many of the people involved with the case also continued to live in the Eatontown area. Frank Dangler passed away in 1930 having lived to the ripe old age of seventy-four. The large Dangler family still resides in the Monmouth County area. Peter Hall eventually sold his hotel and it was converted into the town's Boro Hall. The building was torn down in 1966; however a similar building still stands in its place today. The original building where Allen's Saloon stood still stands to this day at the corner of Throckmorton and Highway 35; significantly altered, it is now a tile business. Constable Liebenthal seemed to have given up his job in law enforcement not long after his arrest. However he stayed in the area and lived well passed the turn of the century. *The Red Bank Registry* continued publication until 1991 before finally closing its doors. *The Monmouth Democrat* was not as prosperous; ceasing publication in the 1940's. Both papers have been replaced by *The Asbury Park Press* as the main source of news in Monmouth County. Monmouth Park Racetrack (where Mingo Jack got his name) was closed in the late 1880's. The area where it once stood is now a housing development. The old entrance to the park is now a street named Park Avenue. The new Monmouth Racetrack opened in 1946 and continues to prosper to this day.

Frank Dangler's grave. (Photo courtesy Of author)

About ten years ago a few members of the Monmouth Historical Society did research on the Mingo Jack story for an exhibit that was displayed at the Monmouth County Public library in Manalapan. They attempted to contact some of the living relatives of the Herbert family who still live in the area; however they received no response to their inquiries. Perhaps after all these years the story is still one that invokes memories that would rather not be talked about. The old stage coach road where Angeline was attacked is long gone and the spot between her house and Jackson Brown's house is now covered in woods. Maps Pond was forgotten and slowly filled in, however a small portion of the pond still exists just off Highway 35. Hidden in trees, the pond is out of sight and out of the minds of anyone who drives by the area. With the advent of automobiles, small local jails like the Eatontown Lockup were no longer needed. The Lockup was abandoned in the 1920's but apparently still stood until the 1950's when what was left of it was finally demolished. Today the spot where the Eatontown lockup once stood is hidden in locust trees and brush just off West Street. Walking the area today, even after one hundred and twenty years, you can still sense the presence of Mingo Jack and get the feeling of a crime committed that will never have closure.

Spot where the Eatontown lockup once stood.
The building was located to the left of the photo
near the pine trees. (Photo courtesy of author)

Bibliography

Gillingham, Evan S. and Bilanin, Frank. *The Story of Eatontown*. The Eatontown Tricentennial Committee. 1970

Hudges, Graham Russell. *Slavery and Freedom in the Rural North: African Americans in Monmouth County New Jersey.*

Images of America Shrewsbury.

Kiernan, Mary Ann. *The Monmouth Patent Part 1.* Greater Red Bank voice. 1986

Pike, Helen C. and Vogel, Glenn D.*Images of America: Eatontown and Fort Monmouth.*Archadia Publishing. 1995

Saretzky, Gary D. *Olde Monmouth Times*. Monmouth County Archives. 1999.

Stavek, Kathleen *Monmouth County Historical Association Newsletter*. 1987

Wolff, Daniel. *4th of July, Asbury Park: A history of the Promised Land.* Bloomsbury 2005.

Newspapers

Red Bank Registry
Monmouth Democrat
New York Times
Eatontown Advisor
Asbury Park Press
New York Sun

CPSIA information can be obtained
at www.ICGtesting.com
Printed in the USA
BVHW071213100821
613833BV00008B/1439

9 781450 213202